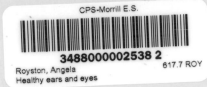

DATE DUE

Look After Yourself

Healthy Ears and Eyes

Angela Royston

Heinemann Library
Chicago, Illinois

Designed by Dave Oakley
Photo research by Helen Reilly
Originated by Dot Gradations Ltd
Printed and bound in China by South China Printing Company

07 06 05 04 03
10 9 8 7 6 5 4 3 2 1

Library of Congress Cataloging-in-Publication Data
Royston, Angela.
  Healthy eyes and ears / Angela Royston.
     v. cm. -- (Look after yourself)
Includes bibliographical references and index.
Contents: Your body -- Your eyes -- Protect your eyes -- Eye tests --
Dust in your eye - Itchy eyes -- Pinkeye -- Your ears -- Take care of
your ears -- Hearing tests -- Earache s-- Protect your ears - It's a fact!.
ISBN 1-4034-4446-3 (Library Binding-hardcover) -- ISBN 1-4034-4455-2 (Paperback)
 1. Eye--Care and hygiene--Juvenile literature. 2. Ear--Care and hygiene--
Juvenile literature. [1. Eye--Care and hygiene. 2. Ear--Care and hygiene.] I. Title.
  RE52.R696 2003
  617.7'06--dc21
                              2003000994

Acknowledgments
The author and publisher are grateful to the following for permission to reproduce copyright material:
Cover photograph by Pauline Cutler/Bubbles.
pp. 4, 22 DK Images; pp. 5, 7 Powerstock; p. 6 Ghislain & Marie David deLossy/Getty Images; p. 8 Trip/Picturesque; p. 9 Anthony Dawton/Bubbles; p. 10 Frans Rombout/Bubbles; p. 11 Adam Hart-Davies/Science Photo Library; p. 12 Jo Makin/Last Resort; pp. 13, 15, 17, 18, 19, 20, 21 Trevor Clifford; p. 14 Mark Clarke/Science Photo Library; p. 16 BSIP, LECA/Science Photo Library; pp. 23, 24 Lucy Tizard/Bubbles; p.25 Eyewire; p. 26 Chris Honeywell; p. 27 Claire Patton/Bubbles.

Special thanks to David Wright for his help in the preparation of this book.

Some words are shown in bold, **like this.** You can find out what they mean by looking in the glossary.

Contents

Your Body 4

Your Eyes 6

Protect Your Eyes 8

Eye Tests 10

Dust in Your Eye 12

Itchy Eyes 14

Pinkeye 16

Your Ears 18

Take Care of Your Ears 20

Hearing Tests 22

Earaches 24

Protect Your Ears 26

It's a Fact! 28

Glossary 30

More Books to Read 31

Index 32

Your Body

Your body is made up of many different parts that work together. Skin, hands, eyes, and ears are just some of these parts.

This girl sees the cat with her eyes. Her ears allow her to hear it purr. This book tells you how to look after your eyes and ears.

Your eyes are **delicate,** so take good care of them! **Eyelashes** and **eyelids protect** your eyes. They help to keep dust and dirt from getting into your eyes.

Some people wear glasses to help them see better. Glasses can protect eyes, too. If you have glasses, make sure you wear them.

Protect Your Eyes

Sunglasses **protect** your eyes from the Sun's rays. These rays can hurt your eyes. Never look directly at the Sun, even if you are wearing sunglasses.

Does the water in a swimming pool make your eyes sting? Swimming goggles help protect your eyes from the water. Goggles also help you see underwater.

Eye Tests

An eye test checks how well your eyes can see. Nurses or **optometrists** test people's eyes. They use special glasses to test each eye.

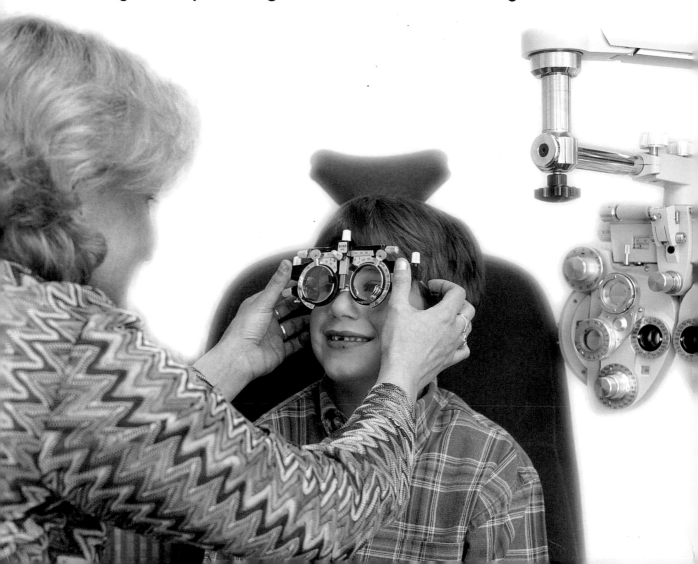

Some people have a hard time seeing things that are close to them. Others have trouble seeing things that are far away. An eye test helps an optometrist decide what kind of glasses you need.

Dust in Your Eye

Sometimes an **eyelash** or a speck of dust gets into your eye. It makes your eye sting and it can really hurt! Blinking fast helps push the speck out.

Your eye makes extra **tears** to get rid of the speck. As you blink, the tears should wash the speck out of your eye. If they do not, ask an adult to help you.

Itchy Eyes

Some people are **allergic** to cats, house dust, or **pollen** from flowers. The fine dust can make their eyes itch. It can make their **eyelids** red and swollen.

Germs can make your eyelids itchy, too. Try not to rub your eyes if they itch. Rubbing your eyes spreads the germs to other parts of your eyelids.

Pinkeye, or **conjunctivitis,** can make your **eyelids** and your eyes red and sore. If you think you may have it, you should go to a doctor.

Pinkeye **germs** spread easily from one person to another. You can even catch pinkeye by using someone else's towel.

Your Ears

Only part of your ear is outside your head.
Most of your ear is inside your head.
Sound travels down the **ear canal** to the **eardrum.**
It goes through the eardrum to the rest of your ear.

There are many **delicate** parts in your ear. They help you hear quiet noises and loud noises. They help you hear noises close-up and far away.

Never put anything except ear plugs in your ears. Ear plugs keep water out of your ears when you swim. Other small things can get stuck in your ear.

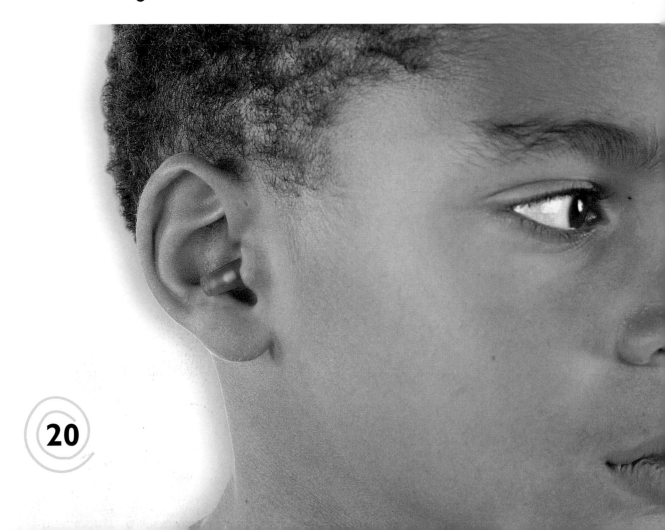

Clean the outside of your ear only. Your ear makes **earwax** to trap dirt. The earwax will slowly come out of your ear by itself.

Hearing Tests

When you go to the doctor for a checkup, you may have a hearing test. Sometimes children have hearing tests at school. It is important to have regular hearing tests.

If you cannot hear well, a **hearing aid** may help you hear better. This boy has a hearing aid behind his right ear.

hearing aid

Earaches

Your ears may ache sometimes if you have a cold or other illness. If the inside of your ear becomes infected with **germs,** it can hurt a lot. You may even feel dizzy.

24

Your parents might give you a **painkiller** to make your ear stop aching. But you should see a doctor. A doctor will look inside your ear and may give you **medicine** to kill the germs.

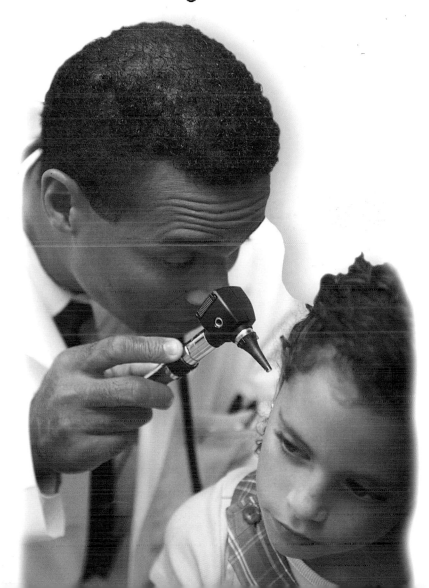

Protect Your Ears

If you are listening through headphones, make sure the music is not too loud. If other people can hear the music from your headphones, then the **volume** is too high. Very loud noises can hurt your ears.

Lower the volume on the television, too. If you listen to very loud noises often, your ears will not be able to hear very quiet noises.

It's a Fact!

Every time you blink, your **eyelid** acts like a windshield wiper—it washes your eye with water.

Blinking is the fastest movement you can make. You blink every few seconds without thinking to cover your eyes with water.

Rubbing your eyes when you have **germs** on your fingers is the most common way of catching **conjunctivitis.** Since you never know when you might have conjunctivitis germs on your fingers, the best way to avoid conjunctivitis is not to rub your eyes!

Sound is measured in **decibels.** People talking normally is about 60 decibels. A CD player played loudly on headphones is about 90 decibels.

Noises that are louder than 90 decibels can hurt your ears. If a loud sound hurts your ears, you should block your ears with your fingers.

People who often work with very loud drills, chain saws, or other loud machines must wear special earmuffs so they will not hurt their ears.

Glossary

allergy   reaction, such as itching or sneezing, by a person's body to things that do not bother other people, such as animal hair, dust, or flowers

bacterium   (more than one are called bacteria) tiny living things. Some types of bacteria can make you sick.

conjunctivitis   infection that makes eyelids and eyes red and sore; also known as pinkeye

decibel   unit used for measuring the loudness of sound

delicate   easily hurt

ear canal   passageway that leads from the outside of your head into the eardrum

eardrum   area of stretched skin inside your head that lets you hear sound

earwax   sticky yellow substance that is made by the skin in the ear canal

eyelash   hair that grows from the edge of the eyelid. It helps keep dirt from getting into the eye

eyelid   fold of skin above and below the eye that partly covers the eye. The upper eyelid opens and closes to uncover and cover the eye.

germ   tiny form of life that causes sickness

hearing aid   small machine with a microphone that makes sounds louder for people who cannot hear well

medicine   substance used to treat a sickness

optometrist   person who gives eye tests and makes up glasses

painkiller   drug that helps to stop pain

pollen   fine dust produced by flowering plants, especially by grasses and some trees

protect   to keep safe

tear   drop of water that spills from the eye

volume   loudness

More Books to Read

Ballard, Carol. *How Do Our Ears Hear?* Chicago: Raintree Publishers, 1998.

Royston, Angela. *A Healthy Body.* Chicago: Heinemann Library, 1999.

Royston, Angela. *Pinkeye.* Chicago: Heinemann Library, 2001.

Index

doctors 16, 22, 25

dust 6, 12, 14

earaches 24–25

ears

  care 20–21, 22,
    24–25,
    26–27, 29

  parts 18, 19

eye tests 10, 11

eyes

  care 6–7, 8–9,
    12–13, 14–15,
    16–17

  itchy 14, 15

  parts 6

  sore 12, 16

germs 15, 17, 24, 25, 28

glasses 7, 11

goggles 9

hearing 5, 19, 22, 23, 27

hearing tests 22–23

noises 19, 26, 27, 29

optometrist 10

pinkeye 16–17, 28

seeing 5, 7, 9, 10, 11

sounds 18, 29

sun 8

sunglasses 8

swimming 9